dinnerlamb

THE AUSTRALIAN Women's Weekly

The problem in planning a book like *Dinner Lamb* is not being able to stop coming up with ideas. Tender, tasty and oh-so-tempting, versatile lamb can star as the main ingredient in countless dishes... no wonder we were spoilt for choice when deciding which recipes to include. We hope you agree that our final selection deserves full marks.

Pamela Clark

Food Director

contents

WEEKNIGHTS

When you're pushed for time, quick-cooking lamb cuts are the answer. From start to finish, all of these dishes can be on the table in less than an hour.

spicy sausage pasta bake

PREPARATION TIME 15 MINUTES **COOKING TIME** 35 MINUTES

Tortiglioni, a straight tubular pasta with grooves on the exterior, works well when baked with a chunky sauce, such as this one. You can substitute it with rigatoni or ziti, if you like, but anything less substantial will get lost amid the hearty sausage and vegetable melange.

375g tortiglioni

6 spicy lamb sausages (900g)

1 medium brown onion (150g), chopped coarsely

1 small eggplant (230g), chopped coarsely

2 medium red capsicums (400g), chopped coarsely

3 small green zucchini (270g), chopped coarsely

700g bottled tomato pasta sauce

½ cup coarsely chopped fresh basil

2 cups (200g) grated pizza cheese

1 Preheat oven to moderate (180°C/160°C fan-forced).
2 Cook pasta in large saucepan of boiling water, uncovered, until just tender; drain.
3 Meanwhile, cook sausages in large non-stick frying pan until just cooked through. Drain on absorbent paper.
4 Cook onion, eggplant, capsicum and zucchini, stirring, in same pan until just tender.
5 Cut sausages into 2cm slices; add to vegetables in pan with sauce and basil, stir to combine.
6 Combine pasta and sausage mixture in deep 3-litre (12-cup) casserole dish; sprinkle with cheese. Bake, uncovered, in moderate oven about 20 minutes or until browned lightly.

serves 6
per serving 36.3g total fat (16.5g saturated fat); 3453kJ (826 cal); 67.7g carbohydrate; 57.6g protein; 7.5g fibre

lamb and rosemary pies with peas

PREPARATION TIME 20 MINUTES **COOKING TIME** 25 MINUTES

1 Heat half of the oil in large saucepan; cook lamb, in batches, uncovered, until browned all over. Heat remaining oil in same pan; cook onion, stirring, until soft. Add flour; cook, stirring, until mixture bubbles and thickens. Gradually add wine, stock, paste and rosemary leaves; stir until mixture boils and thickens. Stir in lamb; cool 10 minutes.

2 Preheat oven to moderately hot (200°C/180°C fan-forced). Oil four holes of 6-hole (¾-cup/180ml) texas muffin pan.

3 Cut two 13cm rounds from opposite corners of each pastry sheet; cut two 9cm rounds from remaining corners of each sheet. Place larger rounds in prepared holes to cover bases and sides; trim any excess pastry, prick bases with fork.

4 Spoon lamb mixture into pastry cases; brush around edges with a little egg. Top pies with smaller rounds; gently press around edges to seal. Brush pies with remaining egg; press one rosemary sprig into top of each pie.

5 Bake pies, uncovered, in moderately hot oven about 15 minutes or until browned lightly. Stand 5 minutes in pan before serving.

6 Meanwhile, heat butter in medium saucepan; add peas, juice and the water, cook, uncovered, stirring occasionally, about 5 minutes or until peas are just tender.

2 tablespoons olive oil

400g diced lamb

4 baby onions (100g), quartered

1 tablespoon plain flour

¼ cup (60ml) dry red wine

¾ cup (180ml) beef stock

1 tablespoon tomato paste

1 tablespoon fresh rosemary leaves

2 sheets ready-rolled puff pastry

1 egg, beaten lightly

4 fresh rosemary sprigs

20g butter

2½ cups (300g) frozen peas

1 tablespoon lemon juice

½ cup (125ml) water

serves 4
per serving 42.7g total fat (18.6g saturated fat); 2868kJ (686 cal); 40.4g carbohydrate; 33.1g protein; 6.1g fibre

lemon and garlic cutlets with broad bean, mixed pea and fetta salad

PREPARATION TIME 30 MINUTES **COOKING TIME** 15 MINUTES

If you can find fresh broad beans, buy about 500g in their pods for this recipe. First, peel them then slit along the rounded back of each bean to remove the hard, grey outer shell. Blanch or microwave the remaining tiny green beans until just tender.

2 tablespoons olive oil

1 tablespoon finely grated lemon rind

2 tablespoons lemon juice

2 cloves garlic, crushed

12 french-trimmed cutlets (600g)

1⅓ cups (225g) frozen broad beans

⅔ cup (80g) frozen baby peas

200g snow peas, trimmed, sliced thinly

1 cup coarsely chopped fresh basil

150g fetta cheese, crumbled

1 cup (150g) seeded kalamata olives

LEMON DRESSING

2 tablespoons lemon juice

¼ cup (60ml) olive oil

1 teaspoon dijon mustard

1 Combine oil, rind, juice and garlic in large bowl; add cutlets, turn to coat in mixture.

2 Boil, steam or microwave beans and peas, separately, until just tender; drain. Rinse under cold water; drain. Peel away grey-coloured outer shells from broad beans; combine beans and peas in large bowl.

3 Meanwhile, place ingredients for lemon dressing in screw-top jar; shake well.

4 Cook cutlets, in batches, on heated oiled grill plate (or grill or barbecue) until browned both sides and cooked as desired.

5 Place snow peas, basil, cheese, olives and half of the dressing in bowl with beans and peas; toss gently. Serve salad topped with cutlets; drizzle with remaining dressing. Sprinkle with a little finely grated lemon rind, if desired.

serves 4
per serving 45.2g total fat (14.9g saturated fat); 2424kJ (580 cal); 17.1g carbohydrate; 27.1g protein; 6.7g fibre

bacon-wrapped chops with baby potatoes in olive pesto

PREPARATION TIME 20 MINUTES COOKING TIME 20 MINUTES

8 loin chops (800g)

4 bacon rashers (280g), rind removed, halved lengthways

⅓ cup (80ml) olive oil

4 medium egg tomatoes (300g), halved

800g baby new potatoes, halved

1 cup firmly packed fresh basil leaves

1 tablespoon lemon juice

¼ cup (60ml) buttermilk

½ cup (60g) seeded green olives

¼ cup (40g) toasted pine nuts

1 Wrap each chop around the outside with one strip of the bacon; securing each with a toothpick.
2 Heat 1 tablespoon of the oil in large frying pan; cook chops, in batches, until browned both sides and cooked as desired. Remove toothpicks, cover chops; stand 5 minutes.
3 Meanwhile, cook tomato in same pan, cut-side down, until soft. Boil, steam or microwave potato until tender; drain.
4 Blend or process remaining oil with basil, juice and buttermilk until mixture forms a smooth paste. Add olives and pine nuts; process pesto until just combined.
5 Place potato and pesto in large bowl; toss gently to combine. Divide potato, chops and tomato among serving plates. Serve with tomato chutney, if desired.

Always press the trimmed basil leaves firmly into a measuring cup so that the proportion of the herb to the other pesto ingredients is correct: too little basil will give the paste a watery texture and a taste that's more of olive than herb.

serves 4
per serving 44g total fat (11.3g saturated fat); 3001kJ (718 cal); 33.4g carbohydrate; 46.8g protein; 6.3g fibre

SKEWERS

Each of these recipes makes eight kebabs; serve with steamed rice or warmed pitta bread, if desired. Soak bamboo skewers in cold water for at least 1 hour before using to prevent them scorching and splintering.

rosemary and garlic kebabs

PREPARATION TIME 20 MINUTES
COOKING TIME 20 MINUTES

8 x 15cm stalks fresh rosemary
1 clove garlic, crushed
1 tablespoon lemon juice
1 tablespoon olive oil
500g diced lamb

1 Pull enough leaves from bottom of rosemary stalks to make 2 tablespoons of finely chopped leaves; toss in small bowl with garlic, juice and oil.
2 Thread lamb onto rosemary stalk skewers; brush with rosemary oil mixture.
3 Cook kebabs on heated oiled grill plate (or grill or barbecue) until browned all over and cooked as desired.

per serving 15.6g total fat (5.7g saturated fat); 1024kJ (245 cal); 0.3g carbohydrate; 26.2g protein; 0.1g fibre

yakitori

PREPARATION TIME 20 MINUTES
COOKING TIME 20 MINUTES

½ cup (125ml) japanese soy sauce
½ cup (125ml) sake
¼ cup (60ml) mirin
2 tablespoons white sugar
500g diced lamb
1 medium carrot (120g), sliced thinly
6 green onions, cut into 3cm lengths

1 Combine sauce, sake, mirin and sugar in small saucepan; bring to a boil. Reduce heat; simmer, uncovered, until sauce reduces by a third. Cool 10 minutes.
2 Meanwhile, thread lamb, carrot and onion, alternately, onto skewers.
3 Cook kebabs on heated oiled grill plate (or grill or barbecue), brushing with half of the sauce occasionally, until browned all over and cooked as desired. Serve yakitori with remaining sauce.

per serving 11.1g total fat (5g saturated fat); 1229kJ (294 cal); 12.1g carbohydrate; 28.4g protein; 1.1g fibre

thai red curry skewers

PREPARATION TIME 20 MINUTES
COOKING TIME 20 MINUTES

2 tablespoons thai red curry paste

1 tablespoon fish sauce

1 tablespoon brown sugar

1 tablespoon lime juice

500g diced lamb

1 medium red capsicum (200g),
diced into 2cm pieces

1 lime, cut into 8 wedges

1 Combine paste, sauce, sugar and juice in
   small bowl.
2 Thread lamb and capsicum, alternately,
   onto skewers; thread one lime wedge on
   each skewer. Brush skewers with half of
   the curry paste mixture.
3 Cook kebabs on heated oiled grill plate (or
   grill or barbecue), brushing with remaining
   curry paste mixture occasionally, until
   browned all over and cooked as desired.

   per serving 14.7g total fat (5.4g saturated fat);
   1124kJ (269 cal); 6.1g carbohydrate;
   27.9g protein; 2g fibre

haloumi and allspice kebabs

PREPARATION TIME 20 MINUTES
COOKING TIME 20 MINUTES

½ teaspoon ground allspice

1 teaspoon cracked black pepper

1 clove garlic, crushed

2 tablespoons lemon juice

2 tablespoons olive oil

500g diced lamb

200g haloumi cheese, diced into 2cm pieces

1 Place allspice, pepper, garlic, juice and oil
   in medium bowl; add lamb, turn to coat in
   mixture. Thread lamb and cheese, alternately,
   onto skewers.
2 Cook kebabs on heated oiled grill plate (or
   grill or barbecue) until browned all over and
   cooked as desired.

   per serving 28.7g total fat (11.8g saturated fat);
   1710kJ (409 cal); 1.5g carbohydrate;
   36.9g protein; 0.1g fibre

chilli rice noodles with bok choy

PREPARATION TIME 20 MINUTES **COOKING TIME** 15 MINUTES

Fresh rice noodles are found in the refrigerated sections of supermarkets as well as in Asian grocery stores. Because they're fresh and not dried, they do not need to be reconstituted by cooking, nor do they require a lengthy soaking time.

400g fresh thin rice noodles

1 tablespoon peanut oil

500g lamb mince

3 cloves garlic, crushed

2 fresh small red thai chillies, chopped finely

400g bok choy, sliced thinly

2 tablespoons tamari

1 tablespoon fish sauce

2 tablespoons kecap manis

4 green onions, sliced thinly

1 cup firmly packed fresh thai basil leaves

3 cups (240g) bean sprouts

1 Place noodles in medium heatproof bowl; cover with boiling water, separate with fork, drain.
2 Heat oil in wok; stir-fry mince until browned. Add garlic and chilli; stir-fry until fragrant. Add noodles, bok choy, tamari, sauce and kecap manis; stir-fry until bok choy just wilts.
3 Remove from heat; stir in onion, basil and sprouts. Serve topped with sliced chilli, if desired.

serves 4
per serving 14.4g total fat (4.7g saturated fat); 1877kJ (449 cal); 44.5g carbohydrate; 34.3g protein; 5.3g fibre

fetta, spinach and prosciutto lamb rolls with herbed kipflers

PREPARATION TIME 20 MINUTES **COOKING TIME** 20 MINUTES

500g kipfler potatoes, halved lengthways

20g butter

1 tablespoon finely chopped fresh flat-leaf parsley

12 slices prosciutto (180g)

20g baby spinach leaves

160g fetta cheese, sliced thinly

4 x 200g pieces backstrap

1 tablespoon olive oil

1 Boil, steam or microwave potato until tender; drain. Toss in large bowl with butter and parsley; cover to keep warm.

2 Meanwhile, slightly overlap three slices of the prosciutto, side by side, on board; layer with a quarter of the spinach, a quarter of the cheese and one piece of the lamb. Starting from narrow end of prosciutto slices, roll carefully to completely enclose lamb. Repeat with remaining prosciutto, spinach, cheese and lamb.

3 Heat oil in large frying pan; cook lamb rolls about 15 minutes or until browned all over and cooked as desired. Cover lamb; stand 10 minutes. Serve lamb sliced thickly with herbed potato and, if desired, a salad of mixed baby leaves.

serves 4
per serving 38.3g total fat (18.4g saturated fat); 2725kJ (652 cal); 16.9g carbohydrate; 60.3g protein; 2.7g fibre

Prosciutto is a kind of Italian ham: salted, air-cured and aged, it is usually eaten uncooked. There are many styles of prosciutto, one of the best being Parma ham, and it's worth it to spend a little more and buy the best quality you can afford.

caramelised onion, pumpkin and lamb pizza

PREPARATION TIME 10 MINUTES **COOKING TIME** 45 MINUTES

Invented in the 1980s by an Italian-American who based his product on a traditional Italian feast-day bread, pre-baked pizza bases are a boon to the weeknight cook. Pitta bread can also be used, and who among us has not made individual pizzas from split English muffins?

1 tablespoon olive oil

2 large brown onions (400g), sliced thinly

600g piece pumpkin, sliced thinly

2 x 335g pizza bases

½ cup (130g) bottled tomato pasta sauce

250g bocconcini, sliced thinly

400g lamb fillets

50g baby rocket leaves

1 Preheat oven to very hot (240°C/220°C fan-forced).
2 Heat oil in medium non-stick saucepan; cook onion, covered, over low heat, stirring occasionally, about 20 minutes or until caramelised.
3 Meanwhile, place pumpkin, in single layer, on lightly oiled oven tray; roast, uncovered, in very hot oven, until just tender.
4 Place pizza bases on oven trays; spread with sauce. Divide cheese and pumpkin between pizzas. Cook, uncovered, in very hot oven about 15 minutes or until pumpkin is browned lightly.
5 Meanwhile, cook lamb, uncovered, in large lightly oiled frying pan over very high heat until cooked as desired. Cover lamb; stand 5 minutes then slice thinly.
6 Serve pizzas topped with caramelised onion, lamb and rocket.

serves 4
per serving 30.1g total fat (12.1g saturated fat); 3733kJ (893 cal); 103.7g carbohydrate; 51.5g protein; 9.8g fibre

barbecued loin chops with creamy mash and flavoured butter

PREPARATION TIME 25 MINUTES **COOKING TIME** 30 MINUTES

Make any one of the following three flavoured butter accompaniments to melt on your chops and serve with our yummy mashed potatoes.

4 large potatoes (1.2kg), chopped coarsely

50g butter

½ cup (120g) sour cream

8 loin chops (800g)

1 Make the flavoured butter of your choice (opposite).

2 Meanwhile, boil, steam or microwave potato until tender; drain. Mash potato in large bowl with butter and sour cream until smooth; cover to keep warm.

3 Cook lamb on heated oiled grill plate (or grill or barbecue) until browned both sides and cooked as desired. Serve lamb with mash and your chosen butter.

serves 4
per serving (without butter)
35.5g total fat
(20.9g saturated fat);
2587kJ (619 cal);
35.4g carbohydrate;
38.8g protein; 4.2g fibre

tamarind and date

1 teaspoon ground cumin

½ teaspoon dried chilli flakes

⅓ cup (80ml) tamarind concentrate

1 cup (160g) coarsely chopped seeded dates

½ cup (110g) firmly packed brown sugar

4cm piece fresh ginger (20g), coarsely grated

½ cup (125ml) water

1 Dry-fry cumin and chilli in heated medium saucepan, stirring, until fragrant. Add remaining ingredients; bring to a boil. Reduce heat; simmer, uncovered, stirring occasionally, about 5 minutes or until thick.

makes 1 cup
per ¼-cup serving (chutney only) 0.1g total fat (0g saturated fat); 698kJ (167 cal); 42.7g carbohydrate; 0.7g protein; 2.3g fibre

rhubarb and apple

1 teaspoon vegetable oil

1 medium brown onion (150g), chopped coarsely

4 cups (440g) coarsely chopped rhubarb

2 medium green apples (300g), chopped coarsely

½ cup (125ml) red wine vinegar

½ cup (125ml) orange juice

¾ cup (165g) caster sugar

1 cinnamon stick

½ cup (80g) sultanas

1 Heat oil in large saucepan; cook onion, stirring, until soft. Add remaining ingredients; bring to a boil, stirring. Reduce heat; simmer, uncovered, stirring occasionally, about 1 hour or until chutney thickens.

tip You need approximately seven large rhubarb stalks for this recipe.

makes 2 cups
per ¼-cup serving (chutney only) 0.8g total fat (0.1g saturated fat); 627kJ (150 cal); 34.6g carbohydrate; 1.6g protein; 3g fibre

tomato and chilli

4 large tomatoes (880g), peeled, chopped coarsely

1 medium brown onion (150g), chopped coarsely

½ cup (110g) firmly packed brown sugar

1 cup (250ml) white wine vinegar

1 tablespoon ground ginger

1 medium green apple (150g), chopped coarsely

½ cup (85g) raisins

1 teaspoon dried chilli flakes

1 teaspoon cracked black pepper

2 tablespoons tomato paste

1 Combine ingredients in large saucepan; bring to a boil, stirring. Reduce heat, simmer, uncovered, stirring occasionally, about 1 hour or until chutney thickens.

makes 2 cups
per ¼-cup serving (chutney only) 0.2g total fat (0g saturated fat); 481kJ (115 cal); 25.9g carbohydrate; 1.8g protein; 2.5g fibre

lamb and quince tagine with pistachio couscous

PREPARATION TIME 20 MINUTES **COOKING TIME** 1 HOUR 30 MINUTES

As with the word casserole, tagine also has two different culinary meanings. Originally from Moroccan kitchens and now found in many of ours, a tagine is the earthenware, cone-lidded vessel in which the spicy, fragrant North African stew with the same name is cooked. The lid serves as a vent, allowing the steam to escape, thus concentrating the flavours of the food inside.

40g butter

600g diced lamb

1 medium red onion (170g), chopped coarsely

2 cloves garlic, crushed

1 cinnamon stick

2 teaspoons ground coriander

1 teaspoon ground cumin

1 teaspoon ground ginger

1 teaspoon dried chilli flakes

1½ cups (375ml) water

425g can crushed tomatoes

2 medium quinces (600g), quartered

1 large green zucchini (150g), chopped coarsely

2 tablespoons coarsely chopped fresh coriander

PISTACHIO COUSCOUS

1½ cups (300g) couscous

1 cup (250ml) boiling water

20g butter, softened

½ cup finely chopped fresh coriander

¼ cup (35g) toasted shelled pistachios, chopped coarsely

1 Melt butter in large saucepan; cook lamb, in batches, until browned. Add onion to same pan; cook, stirring, until softened. Add garlic, cinnamon, ground coriander, cumin, ginger and chilli; cook, stirring, until mixture is fragrant.

2 Return lamb to pan. Stir in the water, undrained tomatoes and quince; bring to a boil. Reduce heat; simmer, covered, 30 minutes. Uncover; simmer, stirring occasionally, about 1 hour or until quince is tender and sauce has thickened.

3 Add zucchini; cook, stirring, about 10 minutes or until zucchini is just tender. Meanwhile, make couscous.

4 Serve couscous with tagine, sprinkled with coriander.

PISTACHIO COUSCOUS Combine couscous with the water and butter in large heatproof bowl, cover; stand about 5 minutes or until water is absorbed, fluffing with fork occasionally. Stir in coriander and nuts.

serves 4
per serving 31g total fat (14.7g saturated fat); 3214kJ (769 cal); 76.7g carbohydrate; 45.4g protein; 12.3g fibre

neck chop and lentil stew with kumara and carrot mash

PREPARATION TIME 20 MINUTES COOKING TIME 1 HOUR 45 MINUTES

1 Cook lentils in large saucepan of boiling water, uncovered, about 15 minutes or until tender; drain.
2 Preheat oven to moderate (180°C/160°C fan-forced).
3 Meanwhile, heat oil in large flameproof casserole dish; cook chops, in batches, until browned. Cook onion, garlic and bacon in same heated pan, stirring, until onion is just browned and bacon is crisp. Add spices; cook, stirring, until fragrant. Add wine, paste, stock and undrained tomatoes; bring to a boil.
4 Return chops to dish; stir in lentils, Cook, covered, in moderate oven 1 hour 10 minutes.
5 Meanwhile, make kumara and carrot mash.
6 Stir coriander into stew just before serving with mash.

KUMARA AND CARROT MASH Boil, steam or microwave kumara and carrot, separately, until tender; drain. Dry-fry cumin in small frying pan until fragrant. Mash vegetables in large bowl with cumin and buttermilk until smooth.

serves 4
per serving 47.9g total fat (19.6g saturated fat); 3896kJ (932 cal); 44.2g carbohydrate; 76.1g protein; 9.9g fibre

1 cup (200g) brown lentils

1 tablespoon vegetable oil

1.5kg neck chops

2 medium brown onions (300g), chopped coarsely

2 cloves garlic, crushed

4 bacon rashers (280g), rind removed, chopped coarsely

1 teaspoon caraway seeds

2 teaspoons ground cumin

½ cup (125ml) dry red wine

⅓ cup (90g) tomato paste

2 cups (500ml) beef stock

425g can diced tomatoes

½ cup coarsely chopped fresh coriander

KUMARA AND CARROT MASH

2 medium kumara (800g), chopped coarsely

2 medium carrots (240g), chopped coarsely

1 teaspoon ground cumin

⅓ cup (80ml) buttermilk

slow-cooked shank and bean ragout

PREPARATION TIME 30 MINUTES (PLUS STANDING TIME) **COOKING TIME** 2 HOURS 30 MINUTES

Haricot and borlotti beans are just two members of the legume family. From the humble baked bean to the chickpea, legumes contain healthy components linked with protection against diseases such as cancer, diabetes and heart problems. They are high in soluble fibre and low in fat, and best of all, they fill you up without filling you out.

½ cup (100g) dried haricot beans

½ cup (100g) dried borlotti beans

8 french-trimmed lamb shanks (1.6kg)

2 tablespoons plain flour

1 tablespoon olive oil

1 large brown onion (200g), chopped coarsely

1 medium carrot (120g), chopped coarsely

1 trimmed celery stalk (100g), chopped coarsely

1 fresh long red chilli, chopped finely

¼ cup (60ml) balsamic vinegar

425g can crushed tomatoes

8 drained anchovies in oil

½ cup (125ml) dry white wine

1 cup (250ml) water

⅓ cup coarsely chopped fresh flat-leaf parsley

1 Place beans in large bowl, cover with water; stand overnight. Rinse under cold water; drain. Place beans in medium saucepan, cover with boiling water; bring to a boil. Reduce heat; simmer, uncovered, about 15 minutes or until beans are just tender. Drain.

2 Preheat oven to moderate (180°C/160°C fan-forced).

3 Toss lamb in flour; shake away excess. Heat oil in large flameproof casserole dish; cook lamb, in batches, until browned. Cook onion, carrot, celery and chilli in same dish, stirring, about 5 minutes or until onion softens. Return lamb to dish with beans, vinegar, undrained tomatoes, anchovies, wine and the water; bring to a boil. Cook ragout, covered, in moderate oven 1 hour, stirring occasionally. Uncover; cook in moderate oven about 1 hour or until meat is almost falling off the bone. Stir parsley through ragout just before serving.

serves 4
per serving 18.1g total fat (6.5g saturated fat); 2077kJ (497 cal); 24g carbohydrate; 54.9g protein; 5.2g fibre